11/10/12.

Joy in many parts of the world is hard to find! Suffering is immense. This book presents the idea that happiness and joy are not one and the same. Because of who Jesus is and what He has done, we may know joy in the midst of struggle.

The proceeds from "True Joy" will go to feed the suffering in Dar Fur, Africa. I have had a tug in my heart for them for several years and decided to print this book as an effort to bring at least some relief. I hope you will join me in this effort!

Dr. Don Lynn

J(True)Y

Dr. Donald R. Lynn

WestBow
PRESS

Copyright © 2012 Dr. Donald R Lynn

All rights reserved. No part of this book may be used or reproduced by any means, graphic, electronic, or mechanical, including photocopying, recording, taping or by any information storage retrieval system without the written permission of the publisher except in the case of brief quotations embodied in critical articles and reviews.

WestBow Press books may be ordered through booksellers or by contacting:

WestBow Press
A Division of Thomas Nelson
1663 Liberty Drive
Bloomington, IN 47403
www.westbowpress.com
1-(866) 928-1240

Because of the dynamic nature of the Internet, any web addresses or links contained in this book may have changed since publication and may no longer be valid. The views expressed in this work are solely those of the author and do not necessarily reflect the views of the publisher, and the publisher hereby disclaims any responsibility for them.

Any people depicted in stock imagery provided by Thinkstock are models, and such images are being used for illustrative purposes only.

Certain stock imagery © Thinkstock.

ISBN: 978-1-4497-6258-2 (sc)
ISBN: 978-1-4497-6259-9 (e)

Library of Congress Control Number: 2012914094

Printed in the United States of America

WestBow Press rev. date: 09/10/2012

Contents

Preface vii
Acknowledgments ix
Introduction xi
Chapter 1 Ode to Joy! 1
               Devotional/Exercise 11
Chapter 2 Anywhere-Everywhere Share! 13
               Devotional/Exercise 23
Chapter 3 A Reason to Rejoice! 25
               Devotional/Exercise 35
Chapter 4 Pressing Toward the Goal—Christ! 37
               Devotional/Exercise 45
Chapter 5 Encouragement to Rejoice! 47
               Devotional/Exercise 55
Afterword 57
Study Guide 59

Preface

My son was only moments ago teaching my firstborn grandson a life lesson about listening. When the task was completed, I mused, *"Now there is a lesson that he will need to learn many more times before his days on earth are done"!* True joy is such a lesson. We have heard the truths this book will give many times, in many ways, but somehow we always need a reminder.

So it is with love! The book of Philippians is all about love. It is about the love of God for people both inside and outside of the community of believers. It is God's love letter written to encourage, inspire, and reclaim the design of God for all of creation and humanity. Through the love of God revealed in Jesus of Nazareth, we discover what it means to be a new creation and the people of God.

Recently I had the opportunity to watch the movies *Flags of Our Fathers* and *Letters from Iwo Jima*. Each story is about soldiers who loved their countries but also loved their families. Each enemy was taught to hate and discount the other. But at the conclusion of the war, many found that their core values were the same. While the geopolitical aspirations of the governments and leaders may have been polar opposites, the values of each soldier were basic to life. The love of life and family was uppermost in their thoughts.

When it was all boiled down to the most basic common denominator, love won out. We will find earth-moving joy when we begin to grasp the unfathomable love God has for each and every one of us and all of us collectively.

Acknowledgments

What a delight it is to be encouraged to write books. From D. Elton Trueblood, to members of my former congregations, to my doctoral colleagues, to most recently a ministry colleague, Dr. Mark Bushor, I have been encouraged to write. However, none of that means more to me than the encouragement of my family, who has listened to my attempts at creativity for decades. They too have recommended from time to time that I should capture my ideas in a print format. This is to thank everyone who has been in my cheering section when my own doubts have remained high. Perhaps now is the time to put a book together—not only for myself but for those who have exhorted me to try.

A special thank you goes to my wife, Mary, who has stood with and by me for thirty-seven years of not only marriage but also ministry. My son, Bryce, and his wife, Keeley, as a ministry couple themselves, demonstrate both joy and love as they work for the expansion of Christ in England. My daughter, Nikki, and her husband, Brian, always challenge me to do my best because they are an inspiration of implementing the principles of true joy each day. Thanks to my grandsons, Cooper, Eli, and Milo, who bring great joy to my life! Thanks also to Clift and Martha King, who not only challenge me to focus on the Lord more than the circumstances but who also have helped resource the publishing of this work.

Introduction

Not every verse of Philippians will be explored in this study, and neither will every theme be developed as an expository explanation of this great work of Paul! Instead the focus is on the primary themes of this letter of adoration. We will see the deep, abiding prayer life that undergirds St. Paul's yearning as a devoted Christ follower.

Thanksgiving exploded from Paul's pen as he reflected on all that a loving God has done and is doing to address the deepest longings of the human experience. Not even the chains of prison damped the exuberant joy that exceeded the routine experiences of many lives—not only in Paul's day but also in ours.

Each new challenge and obstacle to his advancement of the gospel of joy etches the robust thrust of the gospel more deeply into the psyche of the people of God. Forged by the pressures of inner turmoil to turn back or move ahead, his witness is catapulted into the arena of absolute resolve to live in Christlike love and determination. That is what true joy is all about.

People preach for many reasons, but preaching for the pure joy of telling the story of love is what transforms the core of the human experience. Paul knew it! We know it! It is not for power or gratuitous fame. It is for the love of God Almighty that we tell the age-old story of Jesus and his love!

No matter the motive, nothing should exceed the passion to do everything in a way that is worthy of Christ. Everything now reflects him. We reflect adequately or poorly, but reflect him we do. Joy comes in knowing that we have been found worthy of his grace.

In the second chapter of Philippians, we are taken from an exonerated place to the soaring heights of his glorious nature. We find in the second chapter what it is like to live as Christ. We find the whole gospel explained in vibrant, short, and poignant words that cut to the very heart of the matter. It is humbling and revealing for all who read the message.

We also find joy in the companionship of our fellow workers for the gospel. No one lives a Christian life alone. Even when we think we have an original thought, it has already been shaped by mentors, known and unknown. We always stand on the shoulders of our forbearers. I am certainly aware of that as I choose to add my own words to the countless others who have attempted, in the words of the poet Walt Whitman, "to add a verse" or a piece of the good story.

In essence, joy comes from the inside. It is not a veneer that gets embossed on the exterior of a corporeal body. We cannot take confidence in our finitude. It will always keep us wanting and longing for something more pure and long lasting. Our sin nature will always taint our best efforts, but we are admonished to press on toward the goal.

We are challenged to rise above our earthbound existence and allow the power of the resurrection to elevate us to the potential we have in him who has no limits.

What an incredible thing God does in providing us a means to know unfathomable joy. It is not through our own effort but by the work of God that we may possess a new perspective and life. It comes as we—in Paul's words—"await citizenship in heaven and also await a Savior from there"! (Phil. 3:20 NIV 1984)

What a great gift we receive when we allow God to do a perfect work in us that brings us to the precipice of the kingdom of God. It gives us a reason to know *True Joy*!

Chapter 1

Ode to Joy!
Text: Philippians 1:1–2

Most of us have had seasons where regular trips to the mailbox brought a great sense of anticipation—like the anticipation felt by a small child about to be tickled in the hope that laughter will quickly consume the room.

Some of us approach the mailbox with dread. We take tentative, short, cautious steps because of some struggle in our lives or because we anticipate bad news, like jury duty or a bill.

Some travel down long gravel drives to Quonset-shaped containers. Others open brass flaps in their doors. Some walk a half block to a big green box housing sixteen small, locked cubicles. Others have purse-sized metal containers nailed or screwed into the sides of their houses. Each is a receptacle of communication from people we either love or detest.

Most of the time, we bound to the mailbox, wondering what surprise awaits us. We wonder what letter will bring us great joy! Certainly Christmas cards and letters catch us up on what is happening in the lives of our friends and loved ones.

Occasionally, there is a parcel that brightens our day. We know that someone has taken special effort to communicate love and encouragement.

Somehow, mail is more special than an e-mail or a Facebook entry. Even with social networking, there is an anticipation that accompanies what might be delivered to our homes.

We frequently get notes from people we have not heard from in years. We find great delight in hearing about what has happened to them. We often hear about their successes and challenges. Most of them end with the blessing of joy for the season.

The sending and receiving of cards is somewhat like a time of prayer. The writing and reading of notes causes us to pause in the midst of our own schedule to think and reflect. The words that flow from our own pens or desktop computers require conscious thought. It is not automatic. It takes time and effort to say just the right thing.

Paul did this in this letter to the Philippians! He gave us a great gift. As we work through Philippians, we have the opportunity to consider not only what challenged Paul but also our ability to love and express joy. It gives us a chance to express our mood and our present reality.

We give thanks and express joy that, in spite of it all, God has blessed and provided for us in ways beyond our comprehension in abundance when it does not feel like it and in ways we cannot imagine until reflecting on them much later.

The letter to the Philippians is somewhat like a Christmas letter to dear friends. It is a letter of joy! It is a special joy experienced by those centered in the mighty acts of God in Christ. To share in their joy, we must know their Christ! That is right—we must know their Christ! There is no other source for the kind of joy being offered here.

To be truthful, we must admit that we don't always share in the joy of our friends. Every year, I receive a Christmas letter from a family whose children are always number one in their class and captains of the football team or dance troupe. They never seem to have problems. They are absolutely perfect in everything.

Do you know people like this? Do you receive letters like this? The good news in Paul's letter is that it is honest. The church in Philippi had some serious challenges, and so did Paul. The letter was not written to hide or hype the truth. It was an honest exchange of hope, which produces authentic joy.

We may have a hard time understanding this because joy is not about the absence of pain or friction. Yet in the midst of both Paul's ministry team and the church, he found a joy in Christ that moved him beyond myopic preoccupation and spiritual paralysis. By being united in Christ, the Philippians found joy in the face of all their struggles.

What could come in your mailbox that would give you the greatest joy? If you are like many Americans, it would be a sweepstakes entry—or better yet, a confirmation of winning. For many of us, the notice from *Reader's Digest* or Publishers Clearing House Prize Patrol is our greatest desire, because such a prize would allow us to fulfill our wildest dreams.

We believe that joy is a result of having all we have ever wanted. Joy comes with prosperity, success, prestige, and power. Joy, we believe, comes from the outside, not the inside. For many, joy is not even a spiritual matter. It is a material blessing that allows us to do or be whatever we want whenever we want.

Many of us find life so unbearable that we live for our escapist dreams. To many people, joy is the lack of pressure from jobs and families. For some, it is the absence of hardship and peril.

Most believe we don't want a biblical joy that comes in the midst of travail. We want all pain, struggles, and challenges to go away. Knowing that God is with us in Immanuel does not always comfort us. We want Immanuel to resolve the issue or change it for us. We don't want to work through the difficulty and emerge at the place where joy emanates from us. We want God to take care of it for us.

For many of us, to develop this "ode to joy" that Paul described to the Philippians will require a different way of thinking and behaving. That kind of joy will require us to find a new path—a way of being that matches the will of God.

My family and I have watched the mailbox in recent years for more than Christmas cards. My son and daughter, for example, exhibited unusual joy when they were accepted to the colleges of their choice. I confess, Mom and Dad did too! Why? Because we love them. Of course, we had our own dreams, hopes, and plans for them, but the letters symbolized something much deeper than that.

An acceptance letter from a college represents a next step. There is a future and potential to develop a life track that has enormous possibilities. No magic wand has been waved. No full-ride scholarship has been granted. Career guarantees are not sealed. No job is promised upon completion of an academic program. No promises have been made to ensure a trouble-free experience.

Why, then, did we feel joy? Because our children's opportunities allowed them the chance to make choices and decisions that formulated a way of life. They were in environments that forced them to evaluate their belief systems and values. Both had to live their faith in ways that we pray will bring joy to life. A doorway was opened that set a course and a direction.

One definition of *ode,* according to Webster, is "a way or path."[1] I am confident that is what Bryce and Nikki are still finding. I am equally sure that as we unfold this Philippian letter, we will see that more joy comes in defining our paths as congregations and individual believers than in pursuing escapist dreams.

We will also see that this letter is truly an ode to joy. Webster also defines ode as "a lyric or poem addressed to some person characterized by a lofty feeling or dignified style."[2] Philippians is a poetic expression written not just to a person but to all believers with extremely lofty feeling. The challenge to the church will result in dignity and style. A path—a course of action—is clearly revealed. In our union with Christ, we will redefine joy. We will come to understand that joy comes not in the absence of suffering but in spite of it.

We also note that this letter is an ode because of its first two verses. It is a salutation. The salutation reveals who is sending the message, the tone or mood of the sender, and who is to receive it. We can glean a great deal from these short sentences.

The letter begins, "Paul and Timothy, servants of Christ Jesus." It does not begin with a single person but with a team of servants. Later we will learn of others who were on the team as well.

Ministry is not to be done in isolation. The challenges our teams face are usually complex and represent a team of challengers. Even the greatest and most formidable leaders need allegiances and alliances to confront overwhelming odds and situations. Even David, the shepherd boy, joined the Israelite army in the battle.

---

1   *Merriam-Webster's Collegiate Dictionary.* 11th ed. (Springfield, MA: Merriam-Webster, 2003), 519.

2   Ibid., 519.

He took on Goliath, but he teamed with not only the armies of Israel but also with God.

The biblical model is for believers to serve in teams. Jesus sent the disciples out in teams of two or more. We are not to act or serve by ourselves. We find leveraged power by working with a team.

Maybe only at the end of the twentieth century and beginning of this one will we rediscover the joy of teaming with other Christians in the service of our Lord. More has been written in the last five years about transforming ministry teams than in any other time of my ministry.

Even in the work place, the team concept has been institutionalized. From Sony in Japan to Peter Drucker in the United States, we find industry acknowledging the value of teams. Paul did not dream the concept of teams up. He experienced it from the time Ananias partnered with God in laying hands on him to the time Barnabas vouched for his authentic conversion. The team approach was and is the plan of God for the church to extend the joyous message of salvation.

We may hear stories of great leaders like Paul, but he never served alone. People with a variety of gifts surrounded him. Great and gifted givers like Lydia and her band of ladies gave not only hospitality but also great resources to build and extend the church in the world. Philippians was written to thank her and them for participating in the extension ministry of the church.

The salutation tells us the letter is addressed to all the saints, overseers, and deacons. The saints are all those who believe in Christ and have confessed him as the trustee of their lives. The saints become a part of the ode. They have become followers of the path or way of God.

Before believers were called Christians, they were known as the followers of the way, the Word, or the Torah. Their joy came in the ode to Christ. They found their dignity and lofty feelings in uniting in him.

We know from the study of Acts that the church at Philippi began in this union. It was a union of people we may not have expected. You see, some Christians equate joy with successful ministries that grow in numbers and abundant offerings. Some see it as a result of a growing influence in the community. This is not the source or occasion for Paul's joy

Paul was not called to a large synagogue to begin his work in Philippi. He did not convert a large number of Jews or even split this Jewish congregation to extend his work. He and his companions went down by the riverside to pray with a group of ladies. Until this century, there was not even a chapel, a sanctuary, or a building of any kind to mark this place as site for a new community of faith.

Paul did not even find an orthodox Jewish fellowship. He found a group of ladies led by a Gentile God fearer, which simply means one who participated in Jewish worship. Like Jesus did with the Samaritan woman, the ministry team laid the good news of God's love out before them.

The result was the joy of his whole ministry. A church was formed that would face hardship and model faithfulness in the midst of life's most difficult circumstances. From this riverfront meeting was formed the first Asian house or cell church. Lydia's whole family came to Christ. Later Paul's jailer and family would be added. From this unexpected and lowly meeting came a lofty and dignified witness that swept the world. Joy abounded because of their willingness to unite around the evangelical message of Christ, who came to confront the suffering in our lives.

This ode to joy, the Philippian church, became the first building block in the westward expansion of the church. In this fellowship, joy exuded. It could not be contained.

On Thanksgiving eve several years ago in Johnson County, Kansas, Father Ron of the Queen of the Holy Rosary Church shared a marvelous story about his ministry there.

As we ministers tend to do, I asked how his new work was developing. He said that he had some 425 or so in small home groups meeting in his parish. The congregation had grown by 5 percent in the last year.

As he told me this, he had a rather pensive look on his face. An expression of joy swept across it as he suddenly recalled his first days of serving a church. It was not at all unlike the founding of the church in Philippi to which Paul was writing.

Father Ron said he first served a parish in South County. There were no buildings available for mass. He developed a system of home groups where mass and the Eucharist could be observed. He traveled from home to home and developed lay leaders to assist him in the conducting of worship. He had the time of his life because the people were growing in number and in faith.

He said a building was built only because the bishop at the time could not understand how the growth could continue without a physical site to call home. At that point, Father Ron became quiet.

That is when the agenda—the ode, if you will—changed. The focus on small cell fellowships that worshipped God fully and who exercised their gifts for ministry as a team shifted to building a facility. The shift moved from the joy and excitement of seeing the work of heaven accomplished among them to only housing the already gathered. Once that goal was achieved, the evangelistic sharing of God's joy only equaled the number of people the building could hold.

The lesson I learned while hearing this story is the same one we will find unfolding in this letter. Joy comes from a God-directed ode or path, not from our best-laid plans. There is no joy apart from God's plan and purpose accomplished by the mighty acts of God in Christ! The letter charges us to remain Christ centered and God directed.

When joy is often seen from a secular and worldly perspective, which denies the reality of our anxiety and pain, we will need to find the meaning of Christian joy. This is a joy that faces human suffering and unites us in the Christ who sees us just as we are and deals with us.

As we approach this message from the hand of God, we will find a love letter with our names attached. It may say Paul and Timothy, saint or deacon, but be assured you are included. We will find a joy in Christ that is incomparable to the joy of the world. Truly this letter is our ode to joy. In Christ we find our path of salvation.

Devotional/Exercise

Consider where you have been! Where are you coming from?
Consider where you are currently.
Where do you think you are heading?
What brings the greatest joy to your life? How has your
past informed it? How has your present shaped it?
How do you think the Lord of creation
will empower joy in your life?

Prayer

Lord of all that is, create in us a passion for joy! Create
in us a desire to love in ways that truly surprise us.
Give us your heart for the world. Give us what we
need to see priorities and passions as you do.
Give us a path that allows the ode of joy to well up in our souls!
Amen.

Chapter 2

Anywhere-Everywhere Share!
Text: Philippians 1:27—2:4

The dew was heavy on the pasture as we finished our camp cabin duty. Groups of high school students made their way slowly down the dirt road that led to the cinder-block shelter house where chapel was to be held.

Most drug themselves grudgingly to worship, expecting very little. Most had been up half the night talking, planning pranks, and dreaming of relationships that were forming. Most entered the room with an *attitude!*

The topic of the day was the crucifixion of Christ. As the Scripture was read, the scene was reenacted with sound effects. Suddenly all attention was focused on one camper who voluntarily agreed to portray one of the criminals. Each one gasped as he was lifted up to his position next to Jesus. As each graphic detail was explained, the room grew silent.

At the end of the presentation, an assignment was given for each person before the campers were sent out for their daily time of devotions. Without talking, they were to attach themselves or symbolically chain themselves to a person who was tied to a light bamboo cross bar, simulating crucifixion.

They were to meditate on the sacrifice of Christ and the partnership we have with him. For a short period of time, we were riveted poignantly to the reality of suffering connected to the cross of salvation.

Out beyond the shelter house and beyond the dorms was a gently rolling hill. It became a site of transformation. As I crossed the tennis court, I found a young man in tears kneeling on the ground. I asked if he was okay. He only pointed to the hill. From his viewpoint, he could see three crosses with several people attached. In that moment, the whole story made sense. Like Peter before Jesus' trial, he got up and ran away.

Maybe we don't all need to simulate the experience, but we all need to hear the story! We need to share in the suffering of the resurrected Christ. As these students were exposed to pain and suffering, they realized that Christ did so much more for us. Only as they were chained in empathy could they fathom that there would be opportunities to advance the gospel—even in pain.

When life is good and our struggles are few, it can be hard to comprehend or absorb the scope of God's act in the cross. It can seem distant and unrelated until it comes home to us in a life-changing way.

I know that is true for me. I was deeply moved when one of my church couples came to see me about making funeral arrangements. Even while they were in the great pain of grief, they had a loving concern for the state of the souls of their family members.

As we gently and lovingly discussed the wonderful qualities of their loved one, they said, "You need to know that hearts of some of our family members are hard to the gospel. Our hope and prayer is that this time of pain and loss will be a time of softening their hearts."

To some outside of the faith, that may sound harsh or opportunistic. To me it sounded astoundingly loving. Either way, when the gospel is preached, it can be received as good news. That is what this section is all about. Whether we are in chains or suffering the horrendous difficulties of life, our pains may become stepping stones of witness for the salvation of the people God loves.

What we glean from this part of the story is that the good news of God's awesome power and love can be shared in any situation, anywhere. Perhaps it will cost a life, but it can be shared.

The result or harvest is God's work anyway. For many the gospel is heard and received best by those who walk the high road. These are the ones who know the price and walk with integrity and boldness anyway.

Life is good, wholesome, and full of delight. The challenges do not change that. No one can fault a person for finding delight in the goodness and provision of the Lord.

The amazing thing, however, is that God is present even in the hard times. Sometimes we don't know how good God is until we suffer.

Another member of this same congregation found out this truth. Many knew this individual as an extremely devout caregiver and genuinely good person.

Many would automatically put this person in this category. Most don't know the deeper struggles and hardships the person had endured, in part because he always had a positive attitude toward the presenting challenge.

This time, however, he had a health challenge that was evident to many and could not be hidden in self-reliance. It required the healing prayers of friends and colleagues. As I talked with our friend, he shared with me, "I didn't realize how many loving caring people our congregation has. I am blessed to be linked (chained) to so many."

This unfortunate challenge became the occasion for witness and testimony. It was because of Christian compassion that people were motivated to respond. Only in the trial did the opportunity arise to express caring and then to give the Lord credit for it.

Paul's challenge to the Philippians was to preach Christ at all times. The result is the work of the Holy Spirit. Our work is to be awakened to the opportunities that are all about us.

We may think our lives have been too easy and smooth. We have nothing to say. Think again! Give God the praise. You have much for which to thank God. You have been spared trauma and pain, which frees you to focus your life on the advancement of the gospel.

You may say, "I can't give much attention to sharing Christ. I have too much trauma and pain." Think again! Thank God you have been provided an occasion to help others who walk where you walk and watch how you handle the challenges. Your very challenge may be what links or chains you to a person or persons who need only what Christ can give.

Too often we lack the skills or the awareness to turn our opportunity or situation into an occasion for advancing the gospel. This is not to suggest we should take advantage of a person's suffering in a twisted sort of way. It is not to victimize a person who is already suffering. It is to say that as we grow in faith and joy, we want to tell others how we cope and why we hope.

Often it is not even a conscious decision. We automatically call out to God, sing praises, and pray. It is important to hear ourselves say the words. As we find strength, we give encouragement to those around us.

That was true of my parents as they were dying. How they loved to talk with guests and attending caregivers. It was life transforming.

I was told of a nurse whose relationship with Christ had grown cold. Through my mom's faithfulness in dying, the nurse returned to Christ. It changed her negative attitude on the ward and toward life. All of this was because of a conversation she had with my mom as she gave witness to Christ while gasping for breath.

How ashamed I feel at times that I am not more assertive and comfortable in presenting the story. There are times when I realize that I also need to improve my skills and see the opportunities to share—just like most of us. Sometimes I don't willingly link my gifts and witness with others who are giving it their best shot.

There are times when I take the comfort and joy of church life for granted and forget that many don't know the awesome inspiration we have within a vital community of faith. We must all raise our awareness and outreach skill levels just a notch or two by simply telling our stories.

In one church where I served as minister, we did the Contagious Christian event designed by Mark Middleburg from Willow Creek Community Church. About 20 percent or fewer of our church members attended it. We considered it a very successful event and were pleased by the attendance.

For a few weeks, we had a lot of excitement around the church. That year we even had the highest adult conversion rate in recent years. The course helped set faith sharing as a priority.

Being a contagious witness for Christ is not always easy, yet I know I find get joy in seeing a person who is far from Christ establish a new relationship with him. I know that when I don't work at it, my passion grows cold quickly. With all the other issues in my life, my passion to tell my story gets squeezed out. I tend to focus on my pain and my neediness more than on the one who helps me to deal with it.

I also know how many tears streamed down my face a few years ago as I sat in a seminar watching a video of hundreds of people being baptized in churches all over the continent. I know the emotion I felt as people applauded as our own friends parted the waters of baptism in the days that followed.

Not long after the Contagious Christian event, several of us went to Chicago for a leadership event. The purpose of the event was to turn up the heat or passion for evangelism in the lives of our church members. Even so, we know that old habits die hard. I observed that all of us wanted to sit together enjoying each other's company instead of intentionally sitting in areas of the plane where we could develop relationships with people we did not know.

In a flippant sort of way, I made reference to our Contagious Christian event. I said I wanted to give the Contagious Christian Award to the person who brought someone to Christ before we touched town in Chicago. We all laughed and sighed in relief, knowing I was jesting. Besides, after a hard day's work, who would attempt to lead someone to Christ in a short hop from Kansas City to Chicago? After all, we had to center down from the day and focus on rental cars and motels.

Only minutes after we took off, I could hear an excited voice above all the noise of the engines. A man was talking about all the reasons he did not believe in Christ. I listened in because it was a classic rendition of a story line we all hear from time to time. It confirmed that people really do discuss their faith and doubts freely. My thought was who in the world could have gotten this guy so worked up?

As I looked around, I found our youth pastor totally engaged in a passionate conversation with a man whose lifestyle may have held his eternity in the balance. My staff member did not go looking for this opportunity. The Lord presented it to him. It may be interesting to you to know that the man did not make a decision for Christ—that day.

I know the youth pastor learned a lot that night. He learned what he already knew and what he needed to learn to be more effective. I discovered the same. I learned that linking my gifts of prayer with his and teaming overtly in disarming a resistant person might have been more effective than sitting passively by. Beyond that, I learned that the harvest is not ours. It belongs to God.

The harvest will come when it is ready. Who knows what seeds were planted on that day? Some were planted in us. The harvest won't be gathered by itself. We know seeds were loudly broadcast that night. We have no way of knowing the impact on this man or any person in earshot of the conversation. Know the gospel can take root! And in some, it will!

The agitated man had many adversities in his life. Whether he has the seed take root in his life we may never know, but this much I do know: his pains created a new opportunity for me to listen and learn how people think, react, and respond to the gospel. It motivates me to keep on trying and to faithfully share my story and to hone my skills.

Please hear this! With the passion of Paul, I urge you hear that the fields are ripe unto harvest. We live in a vast harvest field where some people are receptive to spiritual truth. What greater joy can we know than for people to know the love of God in Christ Jesus!

Listen to me! On two separate occasions when my kids were in their teens, a monk sharing his faith approached my children. One occasion was in an upscale shopping mall near our home; the other was at an appliance box store. The monk was a Buddhist evangelist sharing his faith in hopes of advancing his philosophy. Do you suppose there is competition out there? Of course there is. I ask you, why do you suppose Buddhism is one of the fastest growing religions in the world? There are two reasons. One is that the convinced are willing to confidently tell their stories. The second is there is a receptive population who is willing to hear and receive it.

What are we to do—say, "Take them, they belong to you. We give up. We forfeit"? I think not. Our children belong to the living God. God has not given them to another. Jesus tells us that he is the truth! He is the way. He is life.

These seeds of truth are to be broadcast wide and far. I can remember as a small boy sitting up until late at night listening to the radio. My brother and I would turn the antenna in all directions to see how far away we could receive a message.

My brother and I were excited as kids when we could pick up WBZ Boston above the static on our old radio. Sometimes we could get the Philadelphia 76ers basketball games. Mostly we got radio evangelists from twenty miles up the road and occasionally from Nashville, Tennessee.

The broadcasting networks were not able to control the airwaves. They simply put their messages out there. Depending on the weather conditions and the quality of the receivers, messages were received by some unlikely people. We can not predetermine the outcome.

Paul knew this too. Even while he was in chains, he was encouraging the church to be bold and to broadcast the good news in every direction and in every situation. Let the Holy Spirit take responsibility for which seeds will take root. We are to use our prosperity and our adversity to benefit the kingdom.

Because Paul was bold, the whole legal system, guards and prosecutors alike, were saved. Families and curiosity seekers were recipients of the good news. All were benefactors. The fruits of their witness came not just in winning the lost but also in encouraging believers.

Skills come by practice and by education. Conversion growth must become normal for the church again! When we are free of chains, we will know joy. In blessing or in adversity, we are to proclaim Christ.

We don't know who is ready to receive Christ, do we? So keep growing, keep learning, keep listening, and keep sharing your life. Someone is watching and listening. In any and every situation, the seed of the gospel may take root.

Devotional/Exercise

Where do you think it would be more comfortable for you to share your faith story? Where would it be most difficult? What must be overcome to allow the story to flow with ease and grace?

Prayer

Lord of all stories, and especially the overarching story of salvation, help us now to speak freely and confidently. We don't want to impose our stories. We don't want to assume the stories of others. We simply want each story to connect to yours. We want to be bathed in the endless grace of your love. We want to rejoice in the true joy that comes when we connect heart to heart!
Amen and amen!

Chapter 3

A Reason to Rejoice!
Text: Philippians 2:5–30

The evening was wearing on after a few days of heavy rains. For days on end, the weather seemingly had created an oppressive blanket for people. Almost all the people I met talked about their irritability and inability to sleep. The downpours and the lighting flashing across the late spring sky kept people on edge. Mary and I felt it too, so we wanted to go sit by Shawnee Mission Lake near our home in Kansas to enjoy a refreshing and sudden shift in the winds and clearing skies.

As we sat on a limestone wall on the north side of the lake, we noticed how comfortable the temperature had become and how the radiant sunlight bounced off of the mirror-smooth lake. It reflected the bright pinks of a beautiful sunset. The oppressive, damp blanket had been tossed back! We felt a new freshness and joy we had not felt for days. We had a reason to rejoice! There had been a change in our circumstances, and we were filled with joy and gladness. The heaviness was gone! We felt a new sense of delight and refreshment. It was like a mini-vacation in the midst of some very heavy realities in our lives.

It is that sense of delight I wish for all of you! Life is so full of heaviness that we need to know there is a reason to rejoice! When we have a fresh experience of the grace of God in Christ Jesus, we have the oppression of life kicked back. It is like a fresh, cool evening wind as it envelops us. We have a reason to rejoice! That is what it is all about!

This passage is like a refreshing reminder of the hope we have in the salvation won for us in Jesus Christ!

The world is so full of oppressing circumstances! The newspaper, Internet news, and broadcast media paint such a grim picture of life. From time to time, we need a reprieve! We need to know that all has not gone south. We grasp and grope for a reason to hope.

Dear friends, we are not without a reason to feel encouraged, supported, and alive to the possibilities of life! We indeed have a reason to rejoice! Because of Christ's victory over sin and death, we have a reason to consider our reasons for rejoicing.

We discover here in this passage that people throughout time have felt what we feel. Know that they have found victory! People have questioned their own faith. They have wondered about the Christian life. Some have felt defeated because they had not yet attained the full maturity of Christ. Some wondered if it was even possible to live the life we are called to live. Doubt reigned supreme in these people's human lives because they had failed to live up to the standard required by Christ.

As a maturing Christian, have you ever had these thoughts and feelings? We feel entombed with them sometimes, don't we? Guilt and fear wraps us up so tightly that we wonder if we can even breathe! Oppressed—yes, we know the feeling. We need a safe place to explore our questions. We also know there are parameters, but it is okay to wonder.

We need a reminder every now and then that we are doing okay! At the same time, we need to be reminded that the Christian life is a process that unfolds the graces of God. We don't achieve perfection in anything instantly and without practice.

I want to kick off the smothering blanket and give you a reason to rejoice! I hope you find my words to be a refreshing, delightful breeze to inspire your attempts to be faithful.

Verse 12 says it just that way: "Continue to work out your salvation in fear and trembling."

While our salvation is sure, it is not complete. Our salvation or wellbeing—that is being well—grows as we grow in our faith and confidence to deploy the power that now resides in us. We have not been left void of power! All power in heaven and earth has been given to those who believe!

To work out our salvation is another way of saying that it is a process. It is never ending and always fresh. As the hymn says, "Morning by morning, new mercies I see. Great is thy faithfulness, O Lord, unto me."

Each and every day we find new reasons to rejoice and give thanks for our blessed relationship with Christ. That is not to say that we always delight in the challenges and issues we face! But we have not been left alone to deal with them or left without empowerment to conquer them.

Hear the powerful truth and reality that gives us the reason to rejoice! "It is God who works in you to will and act according to his good purpose." Philippians 2:12-14 NIV 1984

Hear that God works in you! Maybe we have never really thought about that. God is at work in you! That can be an astounding thought! We often go it alone and try to work as if

God were absent. We believe the deceiver, who tells us that we are powerless and trapped by the circumstances of life.

A pastor friend of mine has been a great blessing to me in this regard. As we pray together on a weekly basis, he thanks God for a second touch of his grace. He often recalls times when he ministered according to his own strength. It almost killed him! He was hospitalized as he was depleted of the energy and resources he needed to serve faithfully.

My prayer mentor said he felt no joy. He felt no passion. He felt no reason to rejoice in the ministry of his calling. After confessing the emptiness of his life, the Lord touched him a second time, and it changed his life. At seventy-plus years old, he is still seeking the grace, forgiveness, and love of the God of our salvation.

He knows now more than ever that he cannot do it alone. He covers everything in prayer and has found a fresh new breeze blowing in his life! My friend knows that God is now at work in him! He knows that he is to do the will of God and act according to it! He has also learned there is a price to pay when we do not. Whenever my mentor drifts from the freshness of God in his life, the deadness returns.

If you are feeling joyless, defeated, and empty, perhaps the next step for you is to confess it. Talk to God! Unburden your heart. Let the truth of life be poured out like a drink offering before God. Hold nothing back. God is awaiting the chance to pull back the oppression from your life so you will be able to rejoice again.

The world knows well the weight of a wet blanket. It awaits a day of liberation. The world is looking for something in which we may rejoice. What better message can we give than to know that God is alive and well and working in us! They need not be just empty words but the verification in the lives of those in whom God is working.

And they need to know for what God is working. God is working in us to do what? "To will and act according to his good pleasure"! Philippians 2:12-14 NIV 1984. How many of us really believe that God wills us good or includes us in life's goodness? So many of us operate out of the opposing position. Many assume that God is an angry, wrathful, unfair, and unjust God. We believe we must work hard to please God or we will pay a heavy price. That denies the loving compassion of God. That is not a pretty or refreshing picture. No rejoicing flows from that scenario. It is a rather bleak and oppressive image.

We must keep the message clear. It is God who is working. God is working to give us a reason to delight and rejoice. Jesus tells us to yoke up with him and our burden will become light.

Too often we become confused and struggle with this notion that we are to do the work. The work is God's to begin with. We are not to ask God to join us in our limited enterprise. We have been invited to join God in the biggest act of liberation anyone can imagine.

Henry Blackaby in his study *Experiencing God:* says exactly that: "See where God is working and go join him. Don't ask God to join you."[3]

Remember that we cannot earn salvation by our works. We rejoice in knowing that we are saved by grace alone. That is the blessing. Salvation does not come by what we do to please God; it comes by letting God's work be revealed in us.

Our work is to do the will of God. We are to get lined up with God and live out the good news in a way that is attractive and winsome.

---

3   Henry Blackaby, Knowing and Doing the Will of God: *Experiencing God* Nashville, Tennessee: Broadman and Holman Publishers 1984, page 121.

For many, the do/done illustration makes this point clear. "Religion is what we do to please God. Christianity is what God has done for us in Christ. In that sense Christianity is not a religion. It is a living relationship with our savior and Lord Jesus Christ." Bill Hybels and Mark Mittelberg, *Becoming a Contagious Christian*, (Grand Rapids, MI: Zondervan, 1994), 223 pp.

This is just another way of saying that we are to act according to God's good purpose. What is that purpose? It is that the world might know God's love manifest in Christ and received as a gift of eternal life that flows from his graceful hands.

We are to know that we do not labor in vain. We have a purpose in life! We have a reason to rejoice! We are an empowered people who will never be separated from the Love of God through Christ our Lord!

As empowered people, we have the word or the key of life for a joyless, lost world! We hold within us the key ingredient to set others free! We may deny it, doubt it, or refuse to turn it, but we have it nonetheless. We even have within our grasp the power to turn oppression into incredible joy and rejoicing!

We are to pour ourselves out with abandon because most do not know the joy and power of being alive to God through Christ. What a different place the world would be if joy reigned supreme!

This is why how we live and act is important. We must reflect the nature of God! The world doubts our message. They want evidence and proof. They want a reason to believe! Understand that they have been given every reason to doubt and wonder.

Do everything without arguing and complaining! That is hard in this season, isn't it? Why? Because arguing and negativity are what our sin nature does! It does not reflect a change in us or demonstrate maturity. It does not suggest that we see new ways of looking at life or dealing with it. It is not attractive to those who are checking out the way of Christ!

Understand that we also live in a crooked and depraved generation. It is a dark blanket in which the refreshing witness to Christ stands out like a beacon.

As children of God, we are to live as blameless and pure people. Why? So we may become an attractive alternative to the oppressive way of the world. Live in such a way that your life is a contrast to the evil, depressing malaise of joyless living.

Remember, we have a reason to rejoice. God is working in us to bring us joy and to provide others with the liberating truth of Christ. We hold the key to the very word of life. It is the key to life for countless numbers of people. We cannot afford to turn them away from salvation because we have not lived in accordance with Christ.

Be encouraged! Receive the admonition to live according to the Spirit of God! Allow others to know the one who now lives in you!

What keeps people from receiving the joyous Word of God? What prevents the rejoicing we are talking about? Positive-thinking gurus say it is attitude! At least with positive thinking we know that improvement can be made. With gospel thinking, we know that the work is not even ours. It is the supernatural will and power of God being done in us that gives hope!

We are, with God's help, to shine like stars against the black backdrop of evil and negativity. The world needs not just words but models. They need to see the truth lived out in real terms, in real time.

It pleases God for us to live in a fresh new relationship of openness and honesty. God was displeased with Adam and Eve because they allowed dishonesty to come between them. They covered themselves and lived a veiled life that was displeasing to God.

It pleases God for us to come to him transparently to live the life designed for us. We are to kick off the blanket of oppression and receive the mantle of joy! We may come unveiled and naked before a loving God who is waiting to embrace us as on the day of our birth.

My daughter Nikki was one who would not stop kicking. Even inside Mary's womb, she kicked and moved about! The nurse would wrap her up tightly to keep her warm, but she would always find a way to kick free! I think she knew there was life out there to be lived, and she did not want to be contained! It was like Lazarus kicking the grave clothes off after being called from the tomb by Jesus.

That is the way life is designed. We are not designed to be bound up and restricted. We are to be set free to live with all gusto and delight in everything life has to offer. We are to be set free from the bondage of sin through the good news of Christ. We are to act and do the good pleasure of God! As we do, we will discover a greater measure of joy. So kick off the oppression of life, rejoice, and be glad! God is at work in you!

Would you agree that we have a reason to rejoice?

Devotional/Exercise

When the wind of the Spirit of God begins to blow, where do you anticipate it will carry you? When you feel free from all that holds you back, what do you want to do? How does it bring joy into your life? How would you joyously participate with God in your world?

Prayer

When the grave clothes of life are full of the stench of death; set us free, Lord. Unbind us and help us kick back the blankets. Hold us. Love us. Help us to be all that is possible so we may live in joy! Amen

Chapter 4

Pressing Toward the Goal—Christ!
Text: Philippians 3:1–21

We live in an interesting time and place as Christians. I wonder sometimes what we have done with the message of Christ and the Word. I want to be careful here. I don't want to demean our brothers and sisters in the faith who draw large crowds or suggest that churches that grow quite large are necessarily in error doctrinally. However, I wonder what mythology we perpetuate in our culture by making superstars or spiritual giants out of church leaders.

If I am honest, I envy at times the success of colleagues who have grown large churches. At times I question their motives. It is a confusing and often thin line between challenging the church to grow and to be authentic while not becoming worldly or theologically thin in the process.

At times I think that many go to mega-churches because they are looking for someone who will tell them everything they need or that every itching ear wants to hear. The assumption is that if a lot of people are going there, then there must be an almost magical or prophetic oracle who may give an answer to my particular challenge. We make the proclaimer a world-class idol or a giant among men.

On the other hand, to be honest, I have been blessed by many of those who have platforms where great numbers of people have come to absorb their teaching.

Herein lies the problem for me and I think for many of us. We begin to believe that these leaders are different than we are. We think they are less tempted, less challenged by daily trials and somehow don't put their pants on just like all the rest of us. We see an image, often of our own making, rather than a servant of God who has a message for us.

I fear we do the same with biblical heroes like Paul, the author of this wonderful love letter that is our subject. Paul was one who preached to crowds, not to draw people to himself but to point them to Christ Jesus, who has done the most wonderful thing.

Even Jesus, I believe, preferred the quiet of self-reflection and small parties for fellowship more than he did the large gatherings where people came pressing in on him to meet their needs.

When the crowds gathered, it broke Jesus' heart because he saw people who were like sheep without a shepherd. He saw masses of people who were longing for something to matter, something to change their situations. People were simply desperate.

All around the world, people are gathering in great numbers for essentially the same thing. Not all who come are convinced! They are seeking after something to address their emptiness, loneliness, and desperation. They are searching for something that can soothe the pain.

Paul confessed, "I have been where many of you are. I have searched, I have committed horrendous sin. But I have been changed. My spiritual journey has led me from murder to surrender. I desperately want you to know the joy I now have in the grace of Christ."

He said, "It is not hard for me to write to you, friends, because I want to provide for you a safeguard." What was he saying? He was saying if there were no traps and errors in thinking, why would it be necessary to say anything? From his own experience, he knew that we must be protected and prepared to face not only abhorrent behavior but also erroneous thinking. Both lead away from the life offered in the resurrection of Jesus.

Salvation comes not in rituals or ceremonies and liturgies, in human effort, pride, and self-justification, but *only* in the forgiving grace of Jesus. We have confidence in nothing else!

We are not saved by how good we are, how much impact we have made in society, or the significance of our influence on either the church or the world. We are saved only by the hand of God who has worked it all out on our behalf through the cross of Christ. That is it!

If that were not so, then Paul would have had no need to be confronted by Jesus on the road to murder. He was "a Hebrew of Hebrews" Philippians 3:5 NIV 1984; He was zealous in the persecution of the church. But to what end?

Paul said, "Whatever were gains to me I now consider loss for the sake of Christ. What is more, I consider everything a loss because of the surpassing worth of knowing Christ Jesus my Lord, for whose sake I have lost all things. I consider them garbage, that I may gain Christ." Philippians 3:7-9 NIV 1984

What did it gain me to do what was required by the law? Nothing! The only thing that matters is obedience and fellowship with Christ, who came to me personally. He did not spare me suffering, pain, or even physical death. Instead he gave me grace and forgiveness now and a hope for eternity later.

My first minister of music in Overland Park was one who challenged me theologically. We had wonderful conversations about the direction of the church and what it meant to be faithful in our time. He, knowing that I preached the centrality of Christ, the miracles of Scripture, and mostly the empowerment of Holy Spirit, wondered how I came to that in light of my theological training. I can remember saying to him, "I have found my theological training has not served me well!"

He smiled but at the same point wanted clarification. I said, "I have spent too much time justifying Scripture instead of preaching it; I have spent too much time defending God rather than sharing his love. I have spent too much time placating people instead of instructing them."

I have wondered how people will react when I tell them that I believe the Scripture to be true and not just an allegory. I wonder who will call me to lead them when I tell them that I believe that Jesus is the Son of God who is raised from the dead and not just a good teacher! I wonder who can hear that the Holy Spirit has come in our age to empower us to be the church of Jesus just as much as were those we read about in Scripture. It is for us too!

Some have said that this is an ignorant, immature understanding of Scripture. I can tell you it is what I believe because of what I have experienced. It is far more exciting than living an intellectualized faith. People will only be changed by the very truth of God revealed and lived out—modeled in modern culture because we believe it.

I want what Paul wanted! And I believe it is what most of us want. It was his personal mission statement. He said, "I want to know Christ and the power of his resurrection and the fellowship of sharing in his sufferings, becoming like him in his death, and so, somehow, to attain to the resurrection from the dead" Philippians 3:9-11 NIV, 1984

So many of us are looking to find a way to avoid pain and suffering. We have had enough emotional pain to kill a horse. We have known physical suffering as well. Who in their right minds would want more except those who discover that suffering for the right things has a great reward and that by passing through it, we find everlasting release!

John the revealer said, "Now the dwelling of God is with men, and he will live with them. They will be his people, and God himself will be with them and be their God. He will wipe every tear from their eyes. There will be no more death or mourning or crying or pain, for the old order of things has passed away … I am making everything new!" Revelation 21:1-5 NIV, 1984

Then he said, "Write this down, for these words are trustworthy and true … It is done! I am the Alpha and the Omega, the Beginning and the End. To him who is thirsty I will give to drink without cost from the spring of the water of life. He who overcomes will inherit all this, and I will be his God and he will be my child." Revelation 21:5-6 NIV, 1984

Isn't that awesome! Isn't that worth suffering a bit longer? Suffering without purpose is a living hell, wouldn't you agree? But sharing in the suffering of Christ who overcame death for us is a prize worth pursuing!

We are not to avoid the realities of death and life by looking for escape and panaceas! We are to look at pain, suffering, and death square in the eye and say, "You are not the last word! You have no control over me!" Without Christ, how could that even be possible? There is no other person or religion that can offer that!

What I sense Paul is saying in the third chapter of Philippians is, "I have not already been made perfect! None the less I press on ... He knocked me to my knees! He blinded me so I could see what he had planned for me. When the scales of blindness fell from my eyes, I was a new man. I saw things I could not see before! I was prideful and full of rage and self-righteousness! But now I know I am only one man among many who are still in process. There is still more for me out there to do and to become."

Do you realize how hard it is to confess this? It is humbling to know that you have done horrific things in the name of God, find forgiveness, speak passionately for the opposite side, and still be humble enough to say you were wrong.

Are we able to do that? We feel it is our divine right to be right! We feel we are somehow less of a person or less powerful if we confess we have blown it from time to time. Have you noticed that humility often does not come before being humbled? It is from humility that we are able to turn to the one who addresses our confusion, pain, and suffering.

The image of the potter illustrates this. It is what Paul was talking about! It is also what Zechariah had in mind. The imperfect piece is punched down and remolded until the object is perfect. The perfection of the potter's hand is still in process. Until the time we are called to heaven, we are in the potter's hand.

In Romans Paul said, "Does not the potter have the right to make out of the same lump of clay some pottery for noble purposes and some for common use? What if God, choosing to show ... his power with great patience to human beings who deserve destruction? What if he did this to make the riches of his glory known to us ... both Jews and Gentiles?" Romans 9:21-22 NIV 1984

To attain the full blessing of God, we must face our imperfections and own them. We must surrender to the one who has made us and called us his own.

Isn't that what we are all looking for? Don't we want to be known as his children? We want to be loved, adored, celebrated, and respected as the persons we were designed and envisioned by God to be in the first place.

But there is more! He says, "Forgetting what is behind (All the trauma, struggle, sin, hurtfulness I have caused), I strain toward what is ahead. As a forgiven person; I look to the future and all that God has for me. I press on, he says, toward the goal—of Christ Jesus." Philippians 3: 12-14 NIV 1984

There are not many sporting events that move me to tears, but cross country is one that does. What moves me is the guts it takes for the last-place runners to finish. They have tenacity and do not give up.

Fans cheer the runners on and encourage them, even when they are heaving up their guts. They strain and press on toward the goal line. As each one finishes, people cheer just as much as if they had finished first.

God is doing that for us! We are being cheered and encouraged onward. God is proud of us and wants us to finish strong!

We are to know, "Our citizenship is in heaven." As Paul said, "We eagerly await a Savior from there, the Lord Jesus Christ, who, by the power that enables him to bring everything under his control; he will transform us and our lowly bodies so that they will be like his glorious body." Philippians 3:20-21 NIV 1984

That was Paul's mission! It must be ours if we are to find true joy!

Devotional/Exercise

Toward what are you running these days with all of your effort?
What is so important that you must finish first?
What requires your energy and time?

Prayer

Lord, help us to discover your action plan—whatever that may be! Through it, help us to discover your joy. More than that, open us to the joy of knowing you fully. Help us to stride toward a worthy finish line. Amen.

Chapter 5

Encouragement to Rejoice! Text: Philippians 4:21–23

I can remember standing with Mary, off by ourselves, following the state championship cross country meet. We said to each other, "I can't believe it is all over!" We were surprised by how many times in the season we were moved by the competitive spirit and the drive of the runners to finish the course.

Only one of the runners could finish first. Many had their personal best finishes. All the runners gave it their best shot, and joy abounded. Even those who had a poorer performance than they anticipated or felt frustrated at the result wrestled with finding joy.

I learned a great deal on that day. Some realized that they were there because they had improved through the season and they were contributors to the team all season long. There were no losers on the course that day. Not everyone felt that way, but it was no less true regardless of their feelings.

As we who were not well-conditioned athletes watched the final sprint to the finish line, we were amazed at how much energy and effort can be extended at the end of a long race.

The last spurt of energy is called the kick! When you start a race, you try to get out ahead of the crowd and find your stride. At the end, your objective is to finish strong and pass your closest competitor if possible. The bottom line is that you are to finish as strong as you started.

Paul's final remark to the Philippians was an encouragement to "finish with a kick." You may remember that the title of chapter 1 is "Ode to Joy"! The context of this letter to the Philippians is joy. In all things rejoice, and find joy in Christ! It is the way we began. It is on that note that we end.

Those who finish the race know a level of joy that comes in accomplishments that we who never begin a race will never know. Those who take their marks from Christ begin a journey that is unlike any other we may undertake. At its end, we, like Paul, want to hear the judge, the gatekeeper, the coach, and our Lord say, "Well done, good and faithful servant!" We want to stretch toward the string extended across the finish line. We want the prize of eternity to be ours.

Just like the runners on the team, we strategize and draft and do all we can to assist our teammates to cross the line with us. That is why so much emphasis is placed on age-appropriate ministries these days.

From children's ministries to senior ministries, the desire is for each one to cross the line victoriously. Leadership teams desire with all their hearts to develop ministry opportunities that will help all people cross the final line together with us. We want to place high in the only race that really matters—the race that Paul has been outlining for us here in Philippians.

We can take great joy in Paul's accomplishments. If it were not for his efforts, we would not be believers today. His perseverance and vision for the advancement of the gospel took root in the culture in which he shared it.

We should be encouraged because he "took it to them" as a people. He did not back off of the deflecting influences of his time. Interestingly, many today say that the world is closer to the world in which Paul ran his race than at any time since the church began.

Therefore we can anticipate similar challenges and results in our efforts to extend the message of Christ's love and our potential to share in his kingdom. His joy may be our joy as we determine to start the race and receive encouragement to end with a kick.

We know this is true because the passage says that greetings were coming to the Philippians from the members of Caesar's house. That means the gospel had penetrated the Roman culture. Paul engaged the culture of the empire, and people were saved. We know that it was a broad receptivity. The poor and the rich alike responded. People of power and the powerless alike shared the common voice of Christ and found profound unity.

Jesus entered the scene of human history at God's appointed time. Many sociological elements were all coming together in a perfect configuration for people to receive God's offer of eternity and a lifestyle that was radically different than what they had ever experienced before.

The Roman influence on world evangelism was profound. The fact that centurions (a regiment of one hundred soldiers) had to obey the commander who elected to share his faith with them was astounding. As they left the homeland for battle, they transported their new faith to battlefields of engagement. The gospel spread by virtue of their transport.

The Romans developed a system of peacekeeping that enabled the missionaries to travel more safely and freely. They had a system of justice that permitted Paul to present the gospel before kings and rulers. All of this is only to say that Paul was a gospel strategist and opportunist. He saw ways to engage the culture and share the good news of Jesus. This is a lesson we need to cultivate in a culture that has just as many lures, traps, and competitive voices as were found in first-century Rome.

How can we truly know joy without seeing the grace in it? Joy is all about God's grace! Do you see how quickly and easily Paul moved from his greeting to his blessing? The blessing is the grace we know in Christ. In this case, Paul was saying that grace means we literally take on the nature of Christ. As we become like him, we become more graceful in the ways we live and work. We extend God's grace to the people who present themselves to us in our lives.

It means that we learn to move more quickly to serve people, to attempt to perceive their points of view and their deepest needs. Our actions are determined by how we determine our best ability to serve. They are determined by how we assess people's relationship to Christ. What is needed that will lead them to or assist them toward the kingdom's doorsteps?

Hear again to whom this message of encouraging grace is sent. It is to all the saints or believers in Christ in the greater Philippian area. Once again, the letter ends with the affirmation of the intent revealed in the beginning. It is not just to an individual that the message of hope and grace is extended. It is given to all who elect to share the kingdom's journey.

After all has been said and done, the message is the same! We are to be a light unto the nations. We are to be beacons of hope and encouragement. We are to be agents of reconciliation and redemption. We are to be a missionary people. We are to search for opportunities to share the good news of Christ to those near and far. One is no nobler or less significant than the other. If the task is to be accomplished, then it will take the best effort of all of us to achieve it.

It takes only a few people to capture the vision and passion for this to turn a church, a city, a nation, and the world. Vivian and George Kovar were two such people in the life of Overland Park Christian Church in Overland Park, Kansas, one of the flagship churches of our denomination in the '60s and '70s. They had a passion for growing the church. In twenty-three years of evangelism calling, they did two thousand calls and five thousand hours of service.

Seventy-five percent of all their calls to invite people to church came through their hands. This was one of the greatest growth periods in the development of this congregation.

Today we have even greater potential in whatever community of faith we participate if we set ourselves about this mission and vision of church within the concept of a team. Most of us are not gifted like Vivian and George were or as passionate. That does not mean we cannot be effective! We must link our spiritual gifts with those who are!

Just as in the church in the first century, we find ways to complement each other's gifts for the purpose of building up the body of Christ on earth. If we have the gift of hospitality, then we should offer to provide a home for a cell group where people may safely explore their faith. If you have a mercy gift, offer it in way that someone may ask you why you serve as you do. If you have a teaching gift, then help as many as you can to understand the grace that comes in knowing Christ.

When each of us use our Holy Spirit–given gifts, we stand together in the presentation of the gospel and the building of

God's kingdom. The world in which this message was shared was full of depravity; religions were failing to meet the expectations of the populace. There was an increasing need for a relationship with a personal God. People needed a Savior to rescue them from the malaise of life. Christ is the answer to that situation.

Does any of that sound familiar? Are we not living in such a world? Are people living in a perverse and depraved world? All I need to do is turn on my computer these days to find out that is so. I received twenty-one e-mail messages recently, fourteen of which were advertisements for pornography. Listen to the news and the subtle messages of radio and TV. There is an erosion of moral and ethical standards.

The religions of the world are not satisfying. People are arriving in church with no historical grounding. There is pain and suffering in their lives. Many who are gathered are seeking answers to life's perplexing questions. People tend not to come to church for the same reasons that people did in the past.

Most people are not looking to make a church their home or to continue their journey of faith in a new town. Oh, some are, but many come to see what a church or religion has to offer. When a need is met, then the search begins anew for a congregation or faith expression that will satisfy the next hunger or craving.

Paul recognized this in his own generation and elected to confront it with the permanent solution that comes in knowing Christ as Lord and Savior. He knew that people need look to no other than Christ. There is no need to look any further. All one needs to do is open oneself to the truth revealed in the life, death, and resurrection of Jesus. He will come and abide in us as we believe in him as Son of God.

It is not about how friendly a church is, however helpful that might be. It is not about growing a church so we have more workers in our children's department or have enough deacons to serve communion on Sunday mornings. It is about the unequaled joy that comes in having a relationship with God through the Son, Jesus. In all of Philippians, Paul's favorite phrase is, "In Christ Jesus"! It communicates his essence and nature.

When we are graced with Jesus' presence, we are to take on that nature for our own lives. It is not a creed to be recited. It is not about church membership or rituals to maintain. To be in him is our life's ambition.

It is not even about us or our deeds. It is about the act of Jesus on the cross and in the resurrection. God is the one who comes seeking to extend grace upon grace to us. To God be the glory!

We end our striving, then, our struggle and conflicts, by finding the Lord's essence emerging increasingly in us. It creates an urging to rejoice and be glad in what the Lord has done and is doing. It is mystical communion, practical empowerment for salvation, cosmic Lordship, and personal relationship with Christ, the Son of God.

People today have a longing for such an opportunity. Salvation can be theirs if we tell the story of grace and offer the opportunity to know the only thing that can ultimately sustain and satisfy. Salvation in Jesus is the answer to our greatest quest. There is an ode, a journey of joy, that is ours in him alone. We must end as we began. We must have one last kick to the finish line. We must live in the joy of the Savior. It is the last great hope of the world!

Devotional/Exercise

What does surrender mean to you? How can we bow before the feet of Jesus and fully grasp what he has done? Are you making life about you? What would happen if you made it about him?

Prayer

How deeply moved we are Lord, by looking once again upon the cross. Our emotions bubble up from the depths of our souls when we are confronted with running a race predetermined by your grace! We can only begin to fathom the incredible depths of your love. What joy must fill your heart when you see that we truly 'get it.' Amen

Afterword

As I come to the end of this work, I realize that my life has moved on. However, I still need the truth of these chapters in my life. Difficulties have continued to come in waves. Career options have come and gone, health challenges have surfaced in my family, and my son and his family have been deployed to the mission work of his calling in England.

It is good to review this material because it reminds me of Paul's words. I am reminded that life is a witness. Before moving on to a new ministry position, I was moved to tears by the comments of a friend in my weekly small group. As the group gathered around my wife and me to pray, he said, "Don, the things you have been enduring have come because you have been faithful, not because you have been unfaithful. In the middle of years of struggle, you and Mary have demonstrated undying faith. Our lives will always be impacted by the way you have faced challenges and continue to seek God's will."

Sometime we don't realize how much the way we live is part of our witness. I have complained and lamented as much as King David. I whine and get angry. I am certainly not superhuman.

In fact, I am very human. I am one who has fallen short of the glory of God. I am one who has been repeatedly broken, and I need a Savior from heaven. I don't know where I would be without him. He is everything to me. I don't deserve his faithfulness, but by grace I have found the one who alone brings unbridled joy and dependability in all matters. Praise be to the God and Father of our Lord Jesus Christ. I am pleased to call him my friend. In him I find *True Joy*.

Study Guide

True Joy: A Study of Philippians! Chapter 1 Student Instructions

Please focus your study on *transformation* more than *information!*

- Listen for the Word of God in transforming Paul and the Philippian Church.
- Listen for how the Lord is transforming you!

Prayer for the Day—say or write a prayer.

Overview

- How we live matters. We become witnesses. We already are witnesses. The question is, are we good witnesses or bad ones for the cause and case of Christ?

- What do our denominational leaders hear about us and our church? What do others in our community hear? Is the grapevine pleasing? Are we standing firm on the foundation of orthodox faith?
- Are we able to identify the enemies for the proliferation of the gospel? What is frightening us? How are we suffering? What difference does the gospel make in real terms and in real time?
- How might we fulfill Paul's joy in our world? The issue is, how do we conduct ourselves in difficult times? How do we deal with life in the face of opposition—political correctness, declining opportunities to share our faith in the workplace—while being a good citizen of heaven and earth?
- Suffering is for the sake of Christ, not our own self-interests.
- The attitude of Christ is the concern for others above self.
- Every knee will bow someday! The great doxology! Jesus is Lord!

Pray:

Assignments beyond Reading:

Write down one thing you will attempt this week from your learning today!

True Joy: A Study of Philippians!
Chapter 2
Student Instructions

Please focus your study on *transformation* more than *information!*

- *Listen for the Word of God in transforming Paul and the Philippian Church.*
- *Listen for how the Lord is transforming you!*

Prayer for the Day—say or write a prayer

Overview

The question of Paul's theology has been raised as it pertains to current issues. For this information to be transformational, we must process the following from a personal experiential perspective, not just a head knowledge.

The simple, straightforward answer is this: Christ! It is all about Jesus! Paul is first and foremost concerned with us knowing Christ. Anything that blocks that pursuit is an issue to be challenged

Second, Paul is about Grace! God forgave him for murder. Who then can stand before a pure and righteous God without it!

- What brings disunity to the body? How do we address it in a way that brings unity? What is needed to bring health, wholeness, and salvation to your community of faith or congregation?
- What lifestyle is required of us to live as Christ does in our world?
- Is your salvation static or developing? Complete or in process? How does salvation impact the congregation? Is it merely personal, or is it corporate?
- How do grumbling, arguing, and gossip impact the church body?

Pray:

Assignments beyond Reading:

Write down one thing you will attempt this week from your learning today!

True Joy: A Study of Philippians!
Chapter 3
Student Instructions

Please focus your study on *transformation* more than *information!*

- *Listen for the Word of God in transforming Paul and the Philippian Church.*
- *Listen for how the Lord is transforming you!*

Prayer for the Day—say or write a prayer

Acknowledge the sovereignty of God first. The work of the Spirit will be evident today in what we do together.

Overview

- What rituals or customs cause you pain to change for the cause of Christ?
- In what ways can you identify with the legalism of Paul, being one who has followed all the rules? What is needed if a rule is broken? What have you put

behind you so you might stretch toward the future to receive even more from the Lord?
- What race are you running right now? How do you know when you have finished or won?

Pray:

Assignments beyond Reading:

Write down one thing you will attempt this week from your learning today!

True Joy: A Study of Philippians!
Chapter 4
Student Instructions

Please focus your study on *transformation* more than *information!*

- *Listen for the Word of God in transforming Paul and the Philippian Church.*
- *Listen for how the Lord is transforming you!*

Prayer for the Day—say or write a prayer

Overview
Torah Questions

- When have you ever had a disagreement with someone in the faith? How did you resolve it?
- Who do you see as a partner in the faith?
- Have you found it easier to find joy in the last few weeks? In what can you now rejoice?
- Do you feel or sense the Lord's nearness?

- What must happen for you to find joy in giving?
- On whom do you depend to provide for your needs?

Pray:

Assignments beyond Reading:

Write down one thing you will attempt this week from your learning today!

True Joy: A Study of Philippians!
Chapter 5
Student Instructions

Please focus your study on *transformation* more than *information!*

- *Listen for the Word of God in transforming Paul and the Philippian Church.*
- *Listen for how the Lord is transforming you!*

Prayer for the Day—say or write a prayer

Overview

- Where do you find encouragement?
- How has God's encouragement of you been communicated in a way that you demonstrate unending joy? Is it through scripture? Or maybe it is the person who loves you? Could it be a person you love? Is it possible you could encourage someone so they too may rejoice in our savior?

Pray:

Assignments beyond Reading:

Write down one thing you will attempt this week from your learning today!

CPSIA information can be obtained at www.ICGtesting.com
Printed in the USA
LVOW111206121012

302505LV00001B/3/P